12 WAYS OF ENLIGHTENED LIVING

NAVIGATING THE COSMIC BALANCE

journey towards bridging the gap between reason and faith

pragati Bangwal

NewDelhi • London

BLUEROSE PUBLISHERS
India | U.K.

Copyright © Pragati Bangwal 2025

All rights reserved by author. No part of this publication may be reproduced, stored in a retrieval system or transmitted in any form or by any means, electronic, mechanical, photocopying, recording or otherwise, without the prior permission of the author. Although every precaution has been taken to verify the accuracy of the information contained herein, the publisher assume no responsibility for any errors or omissions. No liability is assumed for damages that may result from the use of information contained within.

BlueRose Publishers takes no responsibility for any damages, losses, or liabilities that may arise from the use or misuse of the information, products, or services provided in this publication.

For permissions requests or inquiries regarding this publication, please contact:

BLUEROSE PUBLISHERS
www.BlueRoseONE.com
info@bluerosepublishers.com
+91 8882 898 898
+4407342408967

ISBN: 978-93-6783-709-2

Cover design: Pragati Bangwal&Daksh
Typesetting: Tanya Raj Upadhyay

First Edition: January 2025

ABOUT THE AUTHOR

Pragati Bang wal is a renowned yoga instructor and public healer. She supervised 50 NCC students in Dehradun, Uttarakhand. She began her adventure into yoga, meditation, and healing around three years ago. She is now determined to pursue her author career and has written her first nonfiction book, " 12 Ways of Enlightened Living, " which explores the path of cosmic balance.

She is only 28 years old, yet she is very motivated and a positive thinker. Her positivism has cured many people around her. She has the ability to analyse the solution to a certain problem and help those around her overcome a specific difficulty based on a variety of circumstances.

Many individuals have been cured physically, emotionally, and intellectually. As a result, she determined to cure the world by publishing her first book. She also believes that nonfiction books have the power to inspire change and make the world a better place to live .

She enjoys dancing, singing, and writing. She is a health fanatic, adventurous, and enjoys traveling. She began her exploration voyage in her home state of Uttarakhand, Dehradun, and learned a lot along the way. She believed that investigating led to significant enlightenment and healing. Her life 's goal is to make a difference in the lives of others and become well-known for her efforts. She wanted to establish her own identity through herjob, and in the future, she hoped to help the needy and animals by working with non-governmental organisations and orphanages.

Let's follow her on LinkedIn Instagram and youtube - Pragati Bangwal

E-mail. Pragati.bangwal11@gmail.com
Pragati Bangwal.
Dehradun – 248001
E-mail. Pragati.bangwal11@gmail.com

PREFACE

I welcome all readers who decide to read my work. The goal of writing this book is to acknowledge the realities of both science and spirituality. People in this golden era are growing at a rapid speed with a reasonable perspective, leaving our religious culture behind, particularly our younger generation. With the help of this book, I have done my best to convey a message of living a balanced existence by adopting both practical and spiritual minds, which are equally vital. This book is a blend of science and cosmic energy, as well as how these terms relate to one another, based on my own experiences andthe people around me, including my yoga students. I inspired myselfto write this book.

This book will explore and answer every aspect and occurrence that occurs in our lives through various chapters. The fundamental goal of writing this book is to educate people about how the physical world, natural laws, and science function together. In terms of spirituality, we use the term cosmic energy, and science refers to the big bang hypothesis, that we are all aware with. This book aims to inspire readers to believe in science while not neglecting the secrets of the cosmos, which always works in our favour even when we don't grasp its language. This book will describe how modern science emerged from this cosmic energy and is being introduced by our scientists. I believe that research in this field is critical since a non-scientific mind or unholiness among people cannot move or investigate anything beyond the globe. Both fields are dedicated to understanding the nature of reality and our responsibilities in it. This book will teach you the importance of consciousness and manifestation in the physical world. Throughout my life, I've seen how many people struggle with mental health issues in this noisy and modern environment.

Spiritual understanding would assist everyone to overcome various mental disorders . My interest in the secrets of nature and the cosmos began at a young age , despite the fact that my background is spiritual , I was unaware of the term spirituality; instead , I was a person with reasonable thinking who led a practical life until the age of 25. But as we get older , our mental processes alter , and the same is true for me . I've always wanted to make a difference in society , but how? As time progressed, my analysis became more in-depth , and I developed a tendency to learn from my mistakes in life , even the minor ones that caused me grief. Even from my companions , I began checking animals and learning a lot about them and my environment. Now , what prompted me to create this book was the people's limit belief system and their hardships they used to share around. By assessing their situation , I proposed science and spirituality . They simply take a step back from the realities buried in their surroundings and say, "We are modern , or we are science students; we don't understand such things ." I grinned and replied , "Okay , keep going because this is the only reason you are suffering . "And then it occurred to me that publishing a book would be extremely beneficial . Science and spirituality are not mutually exclusive; rather , they are interconnected threads in the same cosmic fabric . This book will provide clarity and understanding into each individual's experience .

In this work, I attempted to cover the fundamental relationship between science and spirituality. I've discussedthe distinction between the two based on my observations. Many authors may have various perspectives depending on their individual experiences. This book will produce a good impact in people's lives by adopting a balanced lifestyle. Many of you may already be aware of these notions. Some may be perplexed, but I have found in our evolutionary world how both a practical as well as spiritual perspective are equally necessary for spreading happiness, love, and peace all around. HARI OM TAT SAT

This book covers all ofthe topics essential to grasp the fundamental concepts of science and spirituality in the greatest way possible.

Pragati Bangwal

TABLE OF CONTENTS

CHAPTER 1
WHAT IS KARMA? INTRODUCTION 1

CHAPTER 2
QUANTUM PHYSICS AND SPIRITUALITY............ 6

CHAPTER 3
TRUSTING THE PROCES 15

CHAPTER 4
UNIVERSE GRATITUDE PRAYER 20

CHAPTER 5
UNIVERSE, MATHEMATICS AND
OBSERVATION... 21

CHAPTER- 6
HUMAN IMPIETY... 29

CHAPTER 7
BOUNDLESS STRENGTH.. 35

CHAPTER -8
UNIVERSEWITHIN.. 42

CHAPTER 9
LIVINGAS A BRIDGE BETWEENWORLDS. 50

CHAPTER -10
THE COSMIC LESSON 54

CHAPTER 11
GLOBALAND PHILOSOPHICAL
 PERSPECTIVES 63

CHAPTER 12
DIVINE MESSAGE: TO EVERYONE 69

ACKNOWLEDGMENT 74

CHAPTER 1
WHAT IS KARMA? INTRODUCTION

Karma is based on our ideas, actions, and the energy we send out and receive, whether good or bad, therefore our karmic accounts should be clear. What I have witnessed throughout my life is that what you sow is what you reap.I am writing this book to acknowledge the importance of balancing practicality and cosmic energy/spirituality for a balanced lifestyle. This is my karma, and the outcome of my actions will be evident.

These are not two distinct terms; rather, they are inextricably intertwined. The purpose of writing this book is to shed light on science and spirituality, as many people have a misunderstanding of these terms and disregard religious principles. Very few people feel that science and spirituality or religion are compatible. I have done my best to explain how the physical world and natural laws work based on the concept of cosmic energy, but only about 20% of scientists believe that most religious people are opposed to science and are so spiritually inclined that they are unable to distinguish between practical and rational thinking.

I am doing my karma with a pure intention, and I am not concerned about the fruit. I am also not sure how many of you will take this book seriously or apply it to your lives after reading it. Whatever happens is the result of a karmic cycle that began not only with this birth but also with prior ones, and we are assigned to families, siblings, friends, and even the place in which we live. In many circumstances, we select a difficult existence to teach the world, and they are elderly souls whose duty is to teach the world by providing an example.

There are situations and circumstances that occur unnecessarily, even if we have not done anything wrong, and we suffer because of our past karma. And after our karmas are cleaned, we tend to understand the source of our pain and begin living a happy life. After acknowledging karma, the karma debt can be eliminated. The concept of karma is very closely tied to Newton's third rule, which maintains that every action has an equal and opposite reaction. This notion is consistent with the concept ofkarma, which holds that every action we take has a consequence, favourable or negative Once we understandthis notion or philosophy, we may apply it to our lives in order to actually become the best version of ourselves and live the most satisfying life possible. When I was in a self-realisation state,I channelized my sufferings that were due to my karma, no matter how small they were. I started clearing my debt of karma, even a single small negative thought, by removing them with my positive actions that brought positive lifestyle with a positive result with 0% suffering, and I started living a blissful life, and now I am in a habit to watch my karmas first if I face even a small suffering, and I am on a stage to work from within because what I believe is to keep our internal world clean and peaceful, once we acceptthis, our outer world can never disturb our inner world and we live a balanced lifestyle, which is what this world really needs inner happiness. The feeling of incompleteness is now complete once we realize ourselves. This is thejourney of self-realization in whichyou work on your flaws and are no longer concerned with changing the world but with changing ourselves. If we change ourselves, the world will automatically change, and this is how positivity works from within. History and events will continue to reoccur until we change our acts or behavior toward that particular situation. **When** I notice recurrent patterns in my life, I enter a meditative state and analyze the situation without blaming anyone, because I am solely responsible for my karma. And what I've noticed so far is that when we work hardto break those recurring patterns, the universe helps us to overcome them. As a result, blaming others, ourselves, or our destiny is foolishness and a lack of knowledge. We can break the cycle by clearing our karmas through experiences and, most importantly, by practicing self-love, being grateful for what we have, and acting and serving those around us with love and forgiveness.

Kindness and acceptance must be practiced in everyday life. There is a need for us to be more mindful of our activities in order to alleviate the pain that this planet is experiencing, specifically a lack of serenity and satisfaction.

"Hello! I am karma,
the law of cause and effect,
A balance that life does perfect.
I give fruits based on deeds
Hence sometimes it is bitter, sour, sweet
Every action, every deed,
Shapes the fate you're destined to lead.
Kindness begets kindness
in return, While cruelty leaves hearts to burn.
The universe keeps a watchful eye,
Ensuring justice, sooner or later will apply.
Hello! I am karma work based
on feelings and thoughts
So, tread the path of righteousness,
For karma's scales bring sure redress.
What you sow, you shall reap.
In this life or another, the cycle will complete.
Hello! I am karma
nobody escaped from my eye,
Embrace love, compassion and care,

For karma's wheel is always fair.
An experience created by you in the universe
My force cannot be neglected, I determined
by your actions, every thought,
every feeling, every word
You will be served what you deserve.
And when shadows of doubt arise,
Trust in karma's eternal guise."

CHAPTER 2
QUANTUM PHYSICS AND SPIRITUALITY

Modern science defines cosmic energy as a light energy that exists everywhere in the galaxy. Reality and consciousness, as I've discovered, are inextricably linked. According to the definition of quantum physics, it is linked in many ways, and from my observations, it is all about consciousness. By being mindful in every element of life in terms of spirituality, we say shakti the creator is manifested in the physical domain. Quantum physics provides insights into the underlying nature of reality ofthe world and natural laws how it operates on the concept of cosmic energy. According to quantum physics, everything is made up of energy and vibrationsWhen one enters the param brahma state, which is the state of attaining supreme consciousness, we become enlightened, receive universal downloading, and get knowledge. Quantum physics has already examined the importance of consciousness in changing reality. Since the last two years, I have been in search of how such things work, and later, I realised that once we align our energy to the universal energy, we get what we want by setting a pure intention, and this is something that people hardly believe. It's okay; everything within you should not be revealed, but if the universe chooses you for a purpose, it will trigger you emotionally, mentally, and physically, and if you stand strong out of these triggers, congratulations. You have passed all of the tests, or the universe is preparing you for difficult battles, which you will win if you trust the process. I was born with a curiosity that led me to investigate the relationship between quantum physics and spirituality, and I attempted to shed light on these two topics.

*Relationship between quantum physics and spirituality:

The convergence of spiritual wisdom and quantum physics creates a compelling framework for interpreting the universe. This concept indicates that underneath the multitude offorms and phenomena lies a unifying force, a rhythm or vibration that works in tandem. For example, when we touch one area of a spider web, the entire web vibrates. In the same manner, our actions and thoughts cause vibrations that affect the cosmos and others around us.

Many hypotheses are based on ancient history. As a modern spiritual practitioner, these analogies are a witness to the wisdom of old spiritual traditions, notably yoga and tantra. Tantra is practiced by spiritual masters, and bhakti Marg is claimed to be the easiest Way to approach deity. Quantum physics and spirituality are similar because both notions explain the nature of our relationships as aware beings to the universe in which we live. My studies began on the day that I began receiving downloads ofthe 5th dimension planet. Being in the 3rd dimension allows one to investigate other realms of the universe. I began researching these concepts and came up the term parallel universe. This theory. Quantum physics also explains astonishing ideas like as parallel dimensions, subtle realities that exist beyond the material world, and fundamental formative fields and energetic structures that serve as matrices for the unfolding and organisation of energy and matter.

*CONCEPT OF 3D, 4D AND 5D

Concept of3D: Objects that can be touched, seen, and felt, as well as everything that surrounds the physical world, are known as 3D. For example, atoms are the smallest indivisible particle of an element that cannot be created or destroyed and are made up of protons, neutrons, and electrons, as we learned in chemistry. People are not fully awakened here; rare people are awakened here and thinking work like they have control over their lives and are surrounded by outer noise, which causes them to fail to follow their instincts that continuously guide us. Their mindset is full of criminal thoughts, and they also outsmart people and try to get an advantage, and mostly they are in their minds. confronts bewilderment, struggles with their lives, separation, disagreements, and all of the other problems we face on a daily basis. This domain is related with materialism, and these are deformed genders trapped in emotional difficulties and ego-driven experiences.

Concept of 4D: What I have observed when my consciousness raised towards this dimension was a change in the diet, self-care, more loving but conscious as well around toxic environment, no more entertainment for those who don't serve better, meditation became a part of my daily routine, even I started teachingyoga that gave me immense pleasure, and my mental health is now my first priority, as well as a desire to pay attention to how my actions affect the environment. A brain with 4D thinking begins to perceive the world through intuitions, or a sixth sense, which grows and expands.

An individual began to seek a deeper meaning in life, and one began to notice synchronicity or the appearance of a magic stick with us, similar to that seen in the Harry Potter film. This is a very sensitive phase because you are aligning with universal energies, so you must monitor your constant thoughts, actions, and feelings,regardless of whether they are positive or negative, because the universe operates on the basis of vibration, which can be against or in favor depending on your thinking frequency.

Therefore, one's intention should be pure. Number synchronicity is the most typical way in which the cosmos communicates with humanity. 4D thinking provides a sense of oneness, and here Nothing is a coincidence. Everything is interconnected; we are simply a component or medium ofit. As I feel compelled to write this book, I am a medium of a cosmos that has chosen me for this purpose. Every person has a unique experience with this world; for me, it was awakening to the idea that we are all connected and that there is more to life than meets the eye. Duality and the concept ofgood and wrong persist, but with greater compassion and understanding.

Concept of 5D: This concept is based on the higher range offrequency. A person with 5D thinking takes responsibility for their emotions; they never blame others if something bad happens to them because they know it is the result of their karma; they chose to serve, do good, and spread love. They have a childish heart, full of passion and creativity. Individuals with a plane of awareness are twisted; they are dissatisfied with their lives, whereas persons with a 5d perspective embrace acceptance. These people are accustomed to good listening abilities.The fifth dimension is something I've been learning a lot about over the last three to four years; it's essentially a plane of consciousness. 5D thinkers have a solid perspective and are guided by inner wisdom. They also guide others using their strong intuitions. Here, passion and purpose are evident. As I previously discussedthe distinction between quantum physics and spirituality,both work on the concept of universal spiritual laws. The same is true for 5D thinkers; they live by universal and spiritual principles. Humans with a 5d perspective understand the nature of 3d and are therefore unaffected by 3rd dimension people. Some such persons are difficult to understand, but they can detect every emotion within a person. They believe in oneness and are linked to the cosmos as a whole; nothing is a coincidence to them. This realm alleviates the fear of death. According to me, a person with 5th dimension thinking that generates slowly or an individual possess by birth includes the first thing he or she feels is connectedness to the self, feeling of oneness, and progress began to develop in an individual's life because he is not bounded with anybody, he will develop his own ideas and will listen to his intuitions that gives the direct path towards the actual purpose of his or life, he started getting clarifications related to lives and surroundings and adopt a tranquil temperament within, and the focus is solely on growth, which is exactly what we all desire. We all desire inner bliss, which only arrives when we start finding answers to everything relating to our life events and also giving solutions to people. Here you will understand the purpose oflife that you have been seeking for so long. You will understand that everyone has their own journey, as do I, and there is a desire to live from a place of pure authenticity. Once you begin operating yourself with the activation of this realm, you will realize that your purpose is to live your truth and seekjoy.

Well, I have a lot to say about this domain; once you realize that there is no rivalry and that there is enough in the Universe for everyone, an overwhelming emotion of love, compassion for life for our mother earth, stars, moon, and joy will emerge. I'm not sure if many of you will believe me, but you will increase your intuition to the highest level and connect with your inner divine and angelic beings. You will automatically start meeting people who share your mindset, which will boost your journey and make you feel like you have butterflies in your stomach.

Higher states of consciousness: There are higher states of consciousness 6,D, 7D, and many more that are possible after we have left our physical bodies, such as possibilities in our meditative state, while sleeping, and dreaming, in which we receive answers about our and other people's lives because that is the state in which you are more connected and your thought power is more activated. A person who is more awake and active may begin speaking less. A person will become more sensitive to loud noises. A higher state of consciousness will keep an individual awayfrom all types of unneeded situations and arguments, as well as situations that are no longer providing a purpose. An individual will receive and tend to grasp the answers he requested from the cosmos, or he prayed for. A person can simply get out of a difficult position if he or she understands the origin ofthe crisis or the conditions around it.

Role of brain waves:

If we turn to our creative side, we can open ourselves to higher awareness. People who think with their right brain are more creative and aware of such worlds. The left brain is logical and analytical, and ifwe balance these two parts, we can do amazing things. 90% of our issues in life will be resolved; we will no longer needto seek advice from others;we will become our own guides, and we will be less stressed, if not zero stress. One can live a progressive lifestyle by combining reasoning with intuition. Higher states of consciousness will result in mystical experiences that are unbelievable to a person dealing with challenges in 3D. "It involves transcending beyond the limitations of the mind and tapping into a deeper sense of connection and oneness with all that exists" This condition provides a profound sense of serenity, clarity, and inner wisdom, allowing individuals to manage life with greater compassion, purpose, and resilience.

My views on Higher state of consciousness

It is possible to acquire this higher awareness through meditation, mindfulness, and self-reflection, allowing us to break free from limiting ideas and patterns and embrace a more rewarding and true way of being.

How one can free from negative and repetitive patterns?

Unfortunately, "freeing oneself requires self -awareness, courage and a willingness to confront and release what no longer serves us, and once we have decided that we have to come out ofthose patterns'things will start working in your favour and the first step is to acknowledge and recognise these patterns observing them without anyjudgment and understanding their root causes"

" Next, we must actively challenge and question these patterns, seeking alternative perspectives and healthier ways ofbeing and responding. With time and consistent effort, we can gradually rewire our minds and habits, replacing old patterns with new, more empowering ones that reflect our highest selves and aspirations.

Coming out ofyour comfort zone and trying new things that bring immense soul happiness, self-talk is very important. Spend at least 10-15 minutes with yourself and analyse your entire day. You are responsible for your actions, accept that, and focus on the present rather than worrying about the future and digging into the past.

CHAPTER 3
TRUSTING THE PROCES

In this evolutionary world, everything evolves with the passage of time. Spirituality has evolved as humans have evolved, and I have observed that it is evolving more than ever, as are our ideas. People are rapidly stepping into quantum physics and neuroscience, and people are experiencing a lot of awakening because nature must balance good and bad. As if nature is telling that the worse will rise and the goodwill awakenPeople are experiencing an awakening process in modernisation because they understand the value of self love and an independent lifestyle; they prioritise self-freedom, and a person with this mindset is incredibly creative, and creativity is the entrance to the universe since it teaches the art of living.

Having faith in life and the journey you are in now it may be clear or may be unclear or paths appear to be more challenging filled with lots of adversities many times or many of you are already going through hard times or tough cycles, in such situation we all are in doubts, negative emotions, heartbroken, everything seems to be ending in such circumstances one should handle the situation patiently by analysing the root cause because being impatient and fear impact the

Trusting in this context involves putting in the effort by visualising and letting go by establishing pure goals, and then returning to your actions by utilising your fundamental life skills and identity traits that will bring us there through determination, discipline, joy, and creativity.

During the lots of hustle and bustle in our life, one should stay calm and surrender towards the particular situation by diverting the mind, or now is the time to meditate and align our thoughts with our inner wisdom that will guide us towards the right path. I always follow this technique, and trust me, it works. Aligning yourselfwith Higher consciousness keeps you stress-free even in your worst situation. People may see it differently or try to bring you down, but ifwe don't react to it, no one can harm us and we stand out strong from that situation because we surrender to the supreme power, relinquishing control of the events and allowing the mystic creation to unfold. We adopt the conviction that everything happens for a reason.Besides, trusting the process calls us to let go ofthe attachments to consequences instead of expectations, and we all need to learn to surrender to the flow of life by trusting that I had a universe continuously guiding me by taking charge of our lives by not giving up on our dreams and on our particular situation because by developing this belief system you will be transformed, by trusting the process we open ourselves to unexpected blessings by being aware that We are being cared for by some favourable energy, and you will undoubtedly notice locked doors opening in your life.

Life is a roller coaster journey of unnecessary sorrows, heartbreaks, encounters with the wrong people, and so on. People with a regular thinking become disturbed by the pains. We suffer because of the karmas we have chosen. However, the effects ofthe karmas we have chosen can be mitigated by filtering our mind, body, and spirit, followed by rituals such as performing and chanting mantras that provide let go and forgiveness.

How can one filter mind, body, and soul?

Shri Krishnaji said in Bhagavad Geeta, "Chinta Chor Chintankar, Chinta Chita Ke saman Hai," whereas self-analysis is the first step towards soul purity and filtration. It is very easy to judge others, but it is very difficultto judge ourselves, so why not judge ourselves rather than others? By judging ourselves, we are one step closer to change from within. The second step toward your growth is waking up in the morning or feeling the want to move your body. I have mentioned a few points of body, mind, and soul filtering. Indulge in a motivational speaker, create positive material, or participate in an inspirational activity such as yoga. Eliminating toxic people from your life may also affect your relationship. Believing that everything around us is energy and we are related to one another, nothing is a coincidence since we are the producers of our lives. Indulge in self-talk. Speak less and do more; action speaks louder than words. Spend 10minutes walking barefoot in the grass to ground yourself.

Perform deep breathing exercises. Spending time in nature will allow your thoughts to flow and help you analyse your current position. Stay in the present.

Empty your mind of old stuck thoughts to allow flow of new concepts.

1. Listen to some spiritual music or recite some Vedic mantras.

Believing in self-realisation and trusting the universe can lead to more ambitious future ambitions for us.

Universal forces always favour a pure heart. Well, there are a few lines I wanted to communicate in writing. I'm not sure why I'm emotional while writing this, and there is a tear drop after each line:

Living my life with this innocent heart

By being kind and praising others

Living my life without any expectations except from myself praising and helping others

I am aware of this roller coaster ride but also, I know deep down Some outer and higher energies are by my side

Oh! Lord embraces me with your grace,

I am your puppet dancing the way you want

I have surrendered to you from that very moment

The time I've realised we all are one and we are connected to one another

Nothing is a coincidence.

Being spiritual by adopting modernism implies discovering your inner power and achieving self-realisation. And this is where we began working on our soul development.

As the elements ofthe cosmos begin to expand with the big bang theory, which we refer to as the cosmic energy womb in spiritual terms, physical evolution begins and continues endlessly, and Earth is the manifestation ofthat cosmic link.

CHAPTER 4
UNIVERSE GRATITUDE PRAYER

"Dear universe with love and grace,
I offer my gratitude to your embrace.
For challenges faced and lessons learned.
My heart is filled with joy, not burned
Through trials and triumphs,
you've held my hand.
Guiding me gently to this precious
land Where love abounds and blessings flow,
And your presence makes my heart glow.
With purpose and compassion,
you light my way Through each passing day,
and every single day.
For your boundless love and infinite grace.
I offer my thanks to the divine space."

CHAPTER 5
UNIVERSE, MATHEMATICS AND OBSERVATION

Many people say that the relationship between universe and maths is very complex because few believe it is Mathematics, and few believe it just a science but what i believe is it is a mixture of rather 3i.e. maths, science and observation. This universe is working based on vibrations and frequencies, we cannot see but we can feel e.g.; Air and this concept is very well explained by Albert Einstein.

Everything is interlinked with one another. Basically, trigonometry is used to calculate distance between planet, stars, galaxies and due to their large distance, they are referred to as light years.

Language of the universe:

To communicate with humans, the cosmos uses numerical signs that must be decoded; this allows us to decipher the secrets, which occurs when the universe's energy flows freely. One can allow energy flow by keeping one's thoughts quiet and noticing what is around them. , Furthermore, by releasing our soul from a limiting belief system and beginning to live life to the fullest by embracing things, our soul is always ready to attain param brahma, which means that when one reaches param brahma, he is disconnected from material life and abandons everything because he is aware of the truth.

Angelic numbers: Also, the cosmos sends some divine numbers to aid us along our path, which is very well articulated by Nikola Tesla. Recognizing patterns and synchronicity, identifying relationships, and measuring uncertainties provides us with useful insights into our surroundings. Some angelic numbers include 11,111,1111, 444,555,936, and so on. The cosmos communicates not just via numbers, but also through signs, symbols, and mediums.

My observations during my journey:

Well, if I share this concept with any of you, people may think I am mad or procrastinating; such things should not be shared, but they exist, and my motive for writing is to explore the truth so that we can live a peaceful life by trusting the process of the universe that it works in our favour. According to my observation higher sources always choose a medium to transmit their messages in order to improve the quality of life on Earth. These figures are merely an inner knowledge that out of nowhere we know that there is something happening that is beyond this worldly world, and there is a sudden alteration in your eating plan Your sleeping and waking up times have improved, you have more energy to do more and more, you have chosen activity over laziness, you are more focused on your career goals, you develop a more giving nature by expecting nothing, you are simply happy from within, and there comes a time when you are more self-loving and self-conscious.. individuals who don't serve you well or are poisonous to you start to disappear, and you start attracting individuals who match your frequency, which happens naturally. You are no longer involved in gossiping and wasting your time on trivial matters.

Numbers that I have come across more frequently were 369. This number was actually trying to get my attention, and when I decoded it, I realised that these numbers form an upper and lower triangle. This number has different meanings depending on an individual's situation. For some, it may be to focus on their thoughts because they are manifesting easily, or you are moving towards abundance, so you must be optimistic.

UPPER TRIANGLE:

The upper triangle depicts the spiritual dimension, which includes our thoughts, beliefs, and higher levels of consciousness.

LOWER TRIANGLE:

Whereas the lower triangle symbolizes the physical world, the realm of our actions, emotions, and material existence. Basically 369is to represent the balance and harmony between these two triangles the union of physical and spiritual world.

The lower triangle symbolises the physical world, which encompasses our actions,emotions, and material existence. Basically, 369represents the balance and harmony between these two triangles, as well as the merger of the physical and spiritual worlds.

CONCEPT OF TRIANGLES:

People may have different perspectives on this, but what I've discovered is that these triangles represent feminine and masculine energies, and their total is 9, which represents the shakti ofthe brahma, the male energy represented by the higher triangle, which is constantly attempting to meet with the brahma. In the spiritual sphere, we worship 9forms of Durga, the Maha Shakti or cosmic energy. This shakti allotted her three forms to Brahma, Vishnu, and Mahesh

Brahma.   < Sarswati

Vishnu.   < Mahalakshmi

Mahesh. < Mahakali

And when these energies united, they brought forth a beautiful creation and balance in the Universe, because creation is incomplete without male and female. The person who realized this notion of life truly understands the Art of Living.

How numbers played a significant role in my life

When I was unaware of the number appearance notion, I simply began exploring and experiencing the number energies they carry. Out of nowhere, I came across with 369. I came to realize this genuinely exists and is introduced by a Nicola Tesla It's an indication that a person is experiencing some important and miraculous changes in their lives, such as sudden urge within me to explore, sudden happiness, and sudden appreciation behavior, which began to develop more loving for our environment and animals. **the numerical energies are:**

NUMBER 6

1. Nurturing

2. Harmony

3. Peace

4. Service to others

If we need to activate number 3 or it is nudging or approaching in our life it carries a positive attribute

1. Creativity

2. Growth

3. Self-expression

4. Communication

5. Self-confidence is essential to success.

6. Displaying your exceptional qualities, talents, and ingenuity to the world without being shy.

7. Be confident when making difficult decisions or undertaking new initiatives.

NUMBER 9

1. Find wisdom in solitude basically self-analysis

2. Some old karmic pattern is releasing, time to accept new beginnings

3. Moving on from toxic situation with a forgiveness

4. Conveys a vibration of love and faith, implying that a judgment or justice is on its way.

5. As a lightworker, you have a natural desire to help others without expecting anything in return. (Save your energy since you can be abused.) Champions against injustice Who will not hesitate to intervene when they witness or experience suffering.

(When the world sends you this number, you're creating rewarding goals.)

What I believe is that once your heart is open and you begin to accept life, when you adopt an accepting attitude, your soul is ready for change, such as a new beginning, new people, a newjob, or a new lifestyle. We may say that the universe chooses us for its mission.

NOTE: Being holiness can sometimes cause suffering because we don't believe in our intuitions and whatever we choose causes us to suffer; however, in such a situation, an individual should never blame anyone for the suffering he or she is experiencing because that soul has awakened and is aware of and accepts the situation he is facing as a result ofthe karma he chose, and through the process of realisation, he is now free ofkarma debt and can begin clearing those karmas.

. . . UNIVERSE IS COMMUNICATING:

1. Falling of objects

2. Through songs – Lines of the song that remind us for something or person

3. Environment is affecting by your emotions

4. Deep inner knowing or deep feeling-felt like this is right, something is wrong, or every part of me wants to do this, that's a clear message from the universe.

5. Through humans (chooses medium)

6. When you get or read a message. Something in a book that deeply resonates with you and you don't know why, but it feels right, and true, it is your inner truth being awakened.

There is a deep truth within us that is linked to universal truth, and when you hear it, something deep within you awakens, causing you to be drawn to it, pay attention to it, and pursue it.

CHAPTER- 6
HUMAN IMPIETY

As a seeker, I frequently wonder, "Why is this?" why things should be this way rather than that, and occasionally I defy social standards because I think something exists that isn't benefiting society as it ought to. We experience and believe all we see in our environment. A human being is pure at birth, but as he grows up, he is exposed to many layers of the world's limited belief system, which impedes the development of his soul. His upbringing and the surroundingshe is in shape his mindset, and for him, that is the reality That way, and occasionally I go against conventional standards because I believe something isn't helping society as it should. Whatever we see in our surroundings, we feel and believe in. When a human is born,he is pure, but as he grows up, he is surrounded by several layers of the world's limiting belief system, which forms a blockage in his soul growth, including the environment in which he is raised. This is how his mentality develops, and it is the truth for him. My belief system is based on my experiences and the realization that there is something beyond the limiting constraints that we face in our lives, and that these constraints are the ultimate source of pain.

Humans with unholiness suffer greatly, for example, from emotional pain, physical pain, circumstances, or a lack of moral purity. It is critical to remember that humans are not defined only by their flaws or sins. Every person is the result of their experiences, beliefs, and problems, and it is only through understanding and empathy that we may bridge the gaps caused by unholiness. Impious individuals confront challenges such as Anger, depression, anxiety, emotional disbalance, lack of intuition, inability to understand their problem, family troubles, lack of emotional intelligence, constant arguing, crime, birth of negativity, lack of confidence, narcissistic behavior, drug addiction, violence, etc

Being holiness can sometimes cause suffering because we are surrounded by such a noisy environment that we fail to listen to our intuitions, and whatever we choose, we suffer. You may also have to suffer in life not because you were bad, but because you did not know when and where to stop being good. A pious being never blames anyone for his acts because deep down that person understandshe is suffering due of his incorrect karma. He chooses to accept the situation and try to analyze how he may solve his pain. He lets go of everything. However, letting go does not imply forgetting; rather, he is more cognizant and prefers mind peace, and by doing so, he has begun to cleanse his karmas and is no longer in anguish. Such people are more focused on issues rather than solutions. They will moan and keep criticising life. They find fault in others and believe they are perfect. They criticize their destiny. Blames the universe for everything. Such people concentrate on problems instead of solutions.These four persons lack inner wisdom and engage in wicked behaviours because They are dissatisfied from within and a victim to bad thoughts, therefore a thought filtration procedure is essential to maintain balance by performing rituals and providing prayers; these are the mind body soul technique purification.These approaches aid in the removal of all grudges, resentments, and a lack of forgiveness, and an individual is free of all the chains that keep us in prison and prohibit us from advancing in holiness. I'm sorry because we're all conscious but remain inspired to grow from within; we're attempting to better those around us and are more focused on their trip than on our own; basically, we're ignoring the truth, which we're aware of.

Let's conclude this chapter by competing with ourselves followed with a Universe Bless Me prayer :

1.*Impurities of impiety beings*:

- Disregard for the Divine: Ignoring or rejecting a higher power, sacred laws, or spiritual practices

- Lack of Inner Morality: A disrespect for spiritual ethics that encourage love, compassion, and oneness

- Ego-Centric Living: Choosing money, power, or selfish goals over spiritual development and community well-being.

- Defying Sacred Principles: Going against characteristics such as honesty, humility, and compassion, which are important to many spiritual traditions

- Dishonoring Sacred Spaces: Misusing or defiling places or objects of devotion

- Apathy Toward Spiritual Practices: Ignoring prayer, meditation, or rituals that connect people to the divine or their higher selves. In my yogicjourney I have observed few clients facing issues who are not pious or disconnected themselves from spirituality and they face such issues like:

Disconnection from Self: A lack of inner tranquility and congruence with one's higher purpose

- Disruption of Collective Harmony: Impiety can cause social strife because moral and spiritual values are the cornerstone of collective wellbeing.

Karmic Impact: According to many spiritual traditions, disrespect and unethical behavior can have bad effects for one's life or soul path.

2. The Path to Reconnection

Spiritual religions highlight that human impiety is not permanent. Restoration can be achieved by self-reflection, which involves acknowledging and understanding the underlying causes of acts .

- Repentance or atonement entails seeking forgiveness, making reparations, and realigning with spiritual principles
- Spiritual practices involve reconnecting with the divine through prayer, meditation, or sacred rites
- Acts of Service: Showing respect for life and others through compassion and kindness.

Human impiety, viewed through a spiritual perspective, serves as a reminder of the delicate balance between reverence and alienation.

While it signifies a breakdown in spiritual harmony, it also provides an opportunity for introspection, growth, and reconnection to the sacred. Individuals and societies can restore harmony and grow spiritually by recognising and confronting impiety.

Let me conclude this chapter by competing against ourselves, followed by a Universe Bless Me prayer.

Universe hear my humble prayer.
Oh! Lord bless me love and care
Enlighten my path with wisdom and light
Strength my spirit as i take each flight
Surround me with your love and
Protect me from harm Empower myjourney,
Restore my energy when I feel weak
Assure my success as my story u seek
Manifest all my abundance that I do
Empower my mission with blessings
from you Illuminate my purpose
and make it shine
Assist me in Aligning my thoughts
And. actions towards you
Bless me to strive for righteousness,
faith,love and peace with those
who have a pure heart,
oh! Lord Bless me not to give up
the battle I struggle every day.
Oh! Lord bless me with your Grace
and light and the rest of the world.

CHAPTER 7
BOUNDLESS STRENGTH

Many experiences of letting go occur while going beyond boundaries and unlimited possibilities. Boundless Leadership is based on the notion of expansion and growth. It embodies the energy ofdesire and progress. Another principle embedded in that one is ; expansion is not straight. It can travel backwards and forwards . Boundless Leadership is an oscillation between boundless possibilities and reconnecting to your basic identity and being. Nature provides the best example for us to learn about the essence of being boundless. Living plants extend to grow. Nature's melody oflife and expansion maybe heard everywhere. It exudes an exhilarating expansiveness. An infinite well of resilience, courage and determination that can help us overcome any obstacle and achieve our greatest dreams. It is a recognition that our true power comes from within, and when we tap into this inner strength, we can accomplish extraordinary things and create a life filled with purpose, passion and fulfillment. "Boundless strength is notjust about physical or mental prowess; it is about the strength of our spirit, the depth of our faith and the unbreakable nature of our souls it is a understanding that we are all connected to a greater power and when we align ourselves with this universal energy, we become unstoppable in our pursuit of happiness and success.

Myjourney towards boundless strength was painful; it took three years from now to overcome emotional and physical pain. I was aware that there is something that I have to concentrate on apart from my studies, and the feeling of incompleteness within me triggered a lot. I realized now is the time for a break from material aspects towards soul growth, the need for self-love and self-priority. I was driven to unlock my creativity, and suddenly I developed an interest in yoga and meditation, and this was the period when I was in a complete blissful condition, feeling fulfilled. from within as if yes this was the thing my soul was craving for, and I started mentoring students and clients and this was the path towards healing not me but everyone around, people benefited a lot from my ideas and my meditative techniques that give ultimate happiness to my soul, and suddenly I started getting more opportunities related to yoga, which was quite shocking to myfamily when I started solving myfamily issues emotionally, mentally, and spiritually, This has always yielded positive outcomes for me. And this time I'm feeling compelled to write, therefore I've discovered an untapped source of strength within myself. The concept of limitless strength refers to having no limitations or restrictions, as well as being large. Omnipotence implies limitlessness. A boundless god has no restrictions or bounds; it transcends all notions, thoughts, rules, principles, and so on. Boundless strength brings you to your best version. Your version of your best self may differ from your family or close friends; therefore, resist the desire to compare yourselfto others. Remember that your concept ofyour best self may evolve over time, so be open to change in all aspects of your life. Having unlimited strength and clarity empowers you to create your own life and make decisions that lead to happiness. Being your best self doesn't always imply winning, but rather recognizing the importance of being up for each task.

Tapping into resilience; one can tap into a boundless strength by assuring the power of self we all carry within. Lack of confidence and not believing in themselves , these kinds of people see nothing worthwhile and therefore do not try to come out oftheir comfort zone . They believe life happens or perhaps they see it as the way it's meant to be. These people have low self –esteem. Maybe because they have been through some failure of some sort that has put them in that condition. A strong sense of self-confidence and self-esteem are essential components.

These qualities allow us to move on in life with power and confidence, rather than doubt. The assurance of oneself provides confidence, courage, and daring to attempt the unattainable, believing that anything is possible. The strength of your personality and character propels you to new heights. A strong personality elevates you two notches beyond your contemporaries and gives you the confidence that boundless heights are within grasp. Self-confidence and belief in oneself are essential components of personal development and success. When we have a strong sense of self, it affects all parts of our lives, impacting our decisions, actions, and attitudes. It boosts our confidence and gives us the strength to take risks, overcome barriers, and follow our dreams.

This power of self is not limited to a chosen few, but rather exists in all of us. It goes above societal expectations, constraints, and misgivings. It allows us to realize our own potential and comprehend the limitless possibilities that are before us. For a long time, I never believed I possessed the self-power, the inner strength that can propel you to greater heights. When I used to see many writers , artists and poets I would wonder how they are able to do such things that I cannot. Until I began to believe in my ability, I began to focus on and improve my capabilities.

Now I am confident in my abilities, inner strength, and skills. This is why I can write, and you can read what I write. The power of self is very important in shaping our lives and achieving success. When we have a high sense of self-assurance, we feel more confident, courageous, and bold. This belief in ourselves enables us to move beyond our comfort zones and undertake tasks that others may consider unattainable. We recognize that with determination and effort, anything is possible. This world is not mostly attracted to you but by your achievements that make you look smarter, confident and independent.

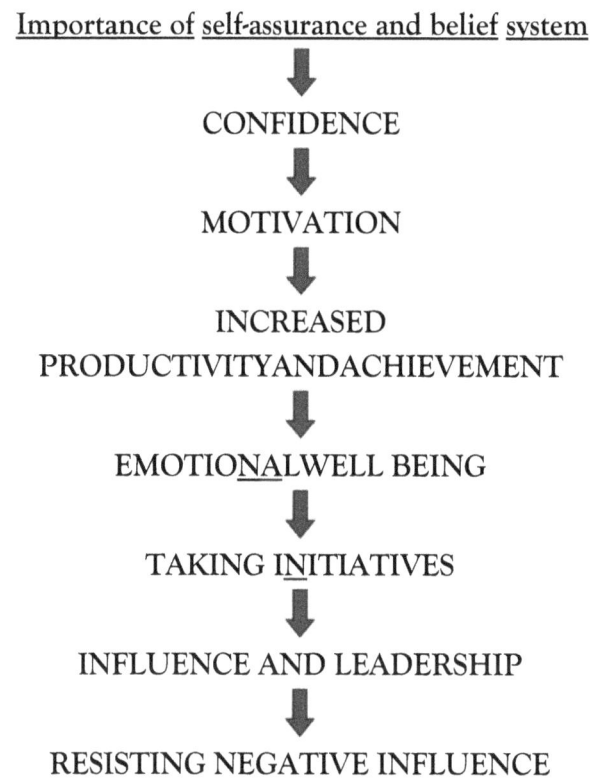

Importance of self-assurance and belief system
⬇
CONFIDENCE
⬇
MOTIVATION
⬇
INCREASED PRODUCTIVITYANDACHIEVEMENT
⬇
EMOTIONALWELL BEING
⬇
TAKING INITIATIVES
⬇
INFLUENCE AND LEADERSHIP
⬇
RESISTING NEGATIVE INFLUENCE

Throughout my analytical period of infinite strength, I discovered a means to tap into inner strength: I began questioning, as mentioned in the previous chapter, which I have a propensity of doing. Why? I make my own decisions. Fortunately, my family members supported myjudgments most ofthe time due to the trust they have in me, I began to practice maintaining cool and self-control in difficulties. In today's society, it's critical to avoid overthinking, let go of negative self-talk, and concentrate on the present. I spend the most of my time with good people who have supported me during some of my most difficult periods. Living a non-regretful existence is the key to unlocking limitless strength.

How it feels when you are urged to tap into your boundless strength?

Let me share with you my feelings and how it feels, sometimes I feel like I can explore the world alone and I have to, sometimes I feel like I can walk miles without any pause, that sounds a bit crazy, a feeling of huge amounts of energy inside and it makes it impossible to concentrate, so basically you are being chosen to do something big and once you are done, you feel a bit relaxed, a feeling of completeness, and I have given a name to this energy, an overflowing energy that needs to be channelised . It is possible to be balanced by splitting and engaging in various duties. By reading, writing, exploring Adventure, workout ,meditation and many more. This is my way to channel my energy and once we work according to the energy channelising technique we live a happy and satisfied life once you set your goals and priorities and start taking actions on that congratulations you are a happy soul. What I have witnessed. Setting specific targets and goals allows us to focus our energies. When we know what we want to do, our energy naturally flows toward that goal. Breaking down huge tasks into smaller, more manageable activities will allow us all to focus and direct our efforts more effectively. The ultimate goal should be to make an attempt to turn weakness into strength and not give up.

CHAPTER -8
UNIVERSE WITHIN

It implies that the universe we view and see is, in fact, a product ofthe mind. I do not mean to deny the existence of a materialistic cosmos. Subjectively, this relates to the cosmos as I view it, which is different from how you perceive it. We all are living in a low density universe which means density of matter is less than the critical density. which means we are living in an open universe that is continuously expanding .

It can also allude to the collective consciousness that unites people, transcending divisions and borders.

Here are various ways to think ofthe universe within:

<u>Interconnectedness:</u> The universe within serves as a reminder of our shared origins and interconnectedness to the universe outside.

<u>Cosmic dancing:</u> The universe within mirrors the cosmic dance that occurs in space.

<u>Self-discovery :</u> Exploring one's own inner universe can lead to self-discovery and cosmic consciousness.

<u>Mirror ofthe universe:</u> The human body reflects the universe's laws, order, chaos, and mysteries.

<u>Personal holiness</u> :I have already discussed this in the previous chapter vibrating higher with a pure intention gives you good results once you ask from yourself

As we know Human body has 5elements :

FIRE, WATER, AIR, EARTH, ESTER

Once we balance these 5 elements in our body we manifest everything in life we want but How?

The five elements are related with the five senses:

Air : is associated with the respiratory system, touch, and motion.

Fire: is associated with digestion, perception, and sight.

Water: is associated with fluid metabolism, taste, and the tongue.

Ether: is associated with sound, the ears, and hollow or empty spaces in the body.

Earth: Associated with scent.

Practice meditation, yoga, and pranayama to assist distribute energy and balance the elements. Be mindful of the elements' natural order: The elements are arranged in the body in the following order: earth and water in the bottom, fire in the centre, and air and space in the top.

Get enough sleep: A steady sleep pattern promotes chi flow(the unseen idea flowing or you can say universal downloading).

Exercise: Yoga,meditation, and tai-chi(cultivating boundless power within) are all good for your body, mind, and spirit.

Spend time in nature: Going on walks might helpyou absorb vitamin D and chi(binding everything together) from your surroundings.

Journal: Writing down your thoughts and feelings can help you to lessen stress.

When Istarted practicing and balancing my 5components,I experienced a rapid shift in my energy level that transported me to a blissful condition. I was doing this unconsciously because I was connected to the universe's automated downloading system, which was guiding me toward my soul purpose. I realized there was something there that needed to be decoded and investigated out of nowhere. I gained an interest in writing and journaling, which brings me great joy because I now realize that my ultimate goal is to be happy, which is what our soul craves.

... My experiences afterfinding balance within:

When I started meditating and nobodyforced me to do this but except my body Lot of emotions and thoughts began to flow, I continued this for 1year and disconnected myselffrom people that doesn't serve me better I started tapping into my creative energy by cultivating a sense of harmony between mind, body

and emotions I started following my emotions.

How I started achieving my inner balance;

1. <u>Self-Awareness.</u> - :

- I started considering my thoughts, feelings and behaviours.

- I started practicing mindfulness in order to notice my condition without any judgment.

- Journaling helped me a lot in processing my feelings and identifying patterns.

2. <u>Setting clear priorities –:</u>

- I started identifying what is important to me
- I started making my daily behavior's consistent with my basic principles and long term goals.

3. *Embraced stillness-:*

- Incorporate meditation, deep breathing, or quiet periods into my daily routine to relax and connect with my inner self.

4. <u>*Physical wellbeing*</u>:

- Eating a well-balanced diet, exercising regularly, and getting plenty of sleep.
- Use yoga to achieve physical and mental balance.

5. Emotional regulation-:

- Recognising and validating my emotions.
- Developed self-compassion and avoid harsh self-criticism.
- started watching motivational quotes and videos.

6.Stay current-:

- Avoided overthinking the past or stressing about the future.
- Focused on the current moment.

7.Healthy boundaries-:

- Learned to say no to commitments that deplete my energy.
- Allowed myselffor relaxation and personal space

8. Nurtured relationships-:

- Surrounded myself with positive and encouraging individuals.
- Communicated frankly and developed genuine relationships.

9.Seek inspiration

- Read, listen, or interact with things that inspire me

- Engage in hobbies or activities that bring me delight.

10.Accepted imperfection

- Recognized that life is dynamic, and balance does not imply perfection • Allowed myselfto adjust and flow with the changes. Inner harmony is a journey, not a destination, and being patient with oneself is essential. Each step I take toward self-awareness and care brings me closer to inner serenity.

People often ask me what is body-mind connection?

I simply answer that our physical body is intricately linked to our inner universe. Sensations, impulses, andbody awareness can help us grasp our inner condition.

This link can be strengthened through practices such as yoga or mindful movement. And also switching to some chanting and meditation mantras.

My personal experiences with the body-mind connection were rather unsettling,but many people have had various situations. I went through an anxiety face attack and I healed it by diverting it towards music healing therapy, and also with body pain ,, severe headache, a constant feeling of being sleepy all the time and a slight heaviness to which I overcome . it by spending time with nature and hanging out with family and friends I started feeling. I began to feel immense gratitude within me, that which generated loving energy, very sensitive towards sensitivity to our environment, empathy and sympathy with for the sufferers. "The universe within is a powerful metaphor for the limitless depths of our inner selves,which include our ideas, emotions, cognition, and spiritual essence. It is enormous, intriguing, and linked, just like the universe outside, providing limitless chances for inquiry and growth." " Understanding and exploring the inner world is critical for selfdiscovery, healing, and harmony. This path allows us to connect with our authentic selves, align with our purpose, and nurture a sense of calm and contentment." Exploring the outer cosmos takes curiosity and daring, whereas exploring the inner universe necessitates self-awareness, introspection, and openness. It is a lifelongjourney in which we embrace both the light and shadow sides of ourselves, ultimately leading to wholeness. The cosmos within tells us that the solutions we seek in the outside world frequently reside within ourselves. By going inward, we can discover boundless potential, strengthen our connection to the universe, and gain the knowledge to negotiate life's complications with grace"I have had personal experience that if I am stuck in any situation, I simply meditate on the solution, I ask for the solution, and I don't know how many ofyou believe it or not, but I immediately receive a solution to the specific problem. My goal in sharing my experiences with you is to build and have faith in the human and cosmic bond."

HOW TO OVERCOME WITH SUCH ISSUES AS IT IS A UNIVERSE CALLING YOUR ENERG YSET ACCORDING TO UNIVERSE RAYS I.E COSMIC RAYS:

Solution: It is wise to investigate both the lifestyle, spiritual, and emotional roots of a certain ailment in order to determine what is causing it. Many times, when we cure the emotional side, the physical ailment naturally disappears.

-Flowing and Aligning- If you're feeling inspired, good, your desires are manifesting, things arejust working, and you have a sense offlow in your life, you're on the correct path.

CHAPTER 9
LIVING AS A BRIDGE BETWEEN WORLDS.

Living as a bridge between worlds entails combining seemingly contradictory aspects of existence, such as the material and spiritual, the personal and the collective, or the rational and intuitive. This position entails navigating life in balance, promoting harmony, and serving as a conduit for insight, growth, and connection. It is a call to embody both pragmatic and spirituality, fusing the tangible and the ethereal.

1.What Does It Mean to be a Bridge?

Dual Awareness: The capacity to retain both material and spiritual perceptions simultaneously

- Connection: Serving as a liaison, interpreter, or harmonizer between disparate realities

- Purposeful Action: Putting spiritual principles into action that benefits both the individual and others.

Example: Someone who their professional ethical workplace.

incorporates spiritual compassion into employment, resulting in a more humane and 2.The Role ofthe Bridge-Builder

1. *Facilitator of Understanding*: Assisting others in seeing the connections between seemingly disparate worlds.

2. *Agent of Balance:* Ensures that neither material nor spiritual issues are overlooked.3. Source of Inspiration: Setting a good example and how harmony can exist amongst different aspects oflife.

3. Challenges of Being a Bridge

Inner Tension: Balancing the demands of two worlds can feel overwhelming.

Misunderstanding: Others may struggle to understand your dual perspective.But trust me once you vibrate higher you started meeting people that matches your vibe and will guide you towards your further goals,they will work as a light in your journey it is our consciousness how we recognise them

Conflicting Expectations: Navigating societal pressures while staying true to your spiritual path.

When I was facing such challenges and still facing I found a solution and that is : To stay grounded in the face of adversity, cultivate selfawareness, patience, and a clear sense ofpurpose.

4. *PrinciplesforLiving as a Bridge Between Worlds*

1.*Embrace Duality*: Recognize that opposites—material and spiritual, light and shadow—are interrelated and necessary for development.

2. *Practice Integration*: Integrate knowledge from one domain into the other, enriching both

3. *Maintain Authenticity:* Stay true to your core ideals while adapting to external situations.

For example -Consider a teacher who incorporates mindfulness practices into standard schooling, combining emotional growth with academic instruction.

4.*Toolsfor Living as Bridges.*

1.Meditation and reflection: Connect with your inner selfto achieve clarity and harmony

2. Community Engagement: Share your knowledge and learn from others to promote mutual improvement

3. Creative Expression: Use art, literature, or other means to express your distinct viewpoint.

Lifelong Learning: Investigate both practical talents and spiritual teachings to broaden your understanding.

The Impact of Living as a Bridge.

Personal Growth: Increased self-awareness, resilience, and fulfillment

- Collective Harmony: Promoting mutual understanding and cooperation among various groups or beliefs
- Global Transformation: Serves as a catalyst for incorporating compassion, ethics,and knowledge into larger societal structures.

6. Vision for the Future

Imagine a world where more people serve as bridges between realms— leaders who combine ethical insight with practical action, communities that combine tradition and innovation, and individuals who balance their inner and outward lives. This vision envisions a future oftogetherness, understanding, and collaborative growth.

Conclusion: Living as a bridge between worlds is both an honour and a responsibility. It needs boldness, adaptability, and a dedication to balancing dualities inside yourself and in the world around you. By accepting thisjob, you become a light of balance, leading people to a more integrated and fulfilling way of life.

CHAPTER -10
THE COSMIC LESSON

The universe itself exemplifies the balance of reason and faith. Stars are formed through measured processes, but their existence elicits awe and wonder that go beyond reasoning. The "cosmic connection" teaches us that various realms are interconnected, moving humanity to greater awareness and unity.

Bridging reason and faith involves recognising their synergy rather than overcoming their differences. Practicality and spirituality, rationality and intuition, science and belief are all interwoven into the global tapestry. By fostering this connection, we align with the universe's greater truth: that matter, and spirit are one harmonious whole. This bridge fosters a life of balance, meaning, and purpose, helping us to comfortably navigate the worlds of reason and faith while remaining grounded in both.

This chapter dives into the tremendous insights provided by the cosmos, demonstrating how these subtopics can lead us to a life of peace, progress, and transcendence.

1. The Universe is a Teacher.

2. A mirror of duality

The cosmos represents the interplay of opposites, such as day and night, creation and destruction, chaos and order .. These contrasts drive life's balance and growth

3. *Patterns of Interconnection*: The universe is interconnected at all scales, from atoms to galaxies

4. *Timeless wisdom:*

- Nature's stars, planets, and cycles impart timeless wisdom on patience, resilience, and adaptability.

5. Accepting Unity in Duality

1. *Duality as Completeness:*

- Just as light requires shadow to define itself, all dualities are necessary for balance.

Wisdom and guidance lies within struggles

1. Nature ofStruggles

A-Universal Experience:

- Struggles are part ofthe humanjourney, bringing us together in common challenges
- They can take different forms, including emotional, physical, spiritual, and relational

2. Growth Drivers

- Struggles push us to adapt and evolve
- They encourage self-reflection and highlight areas for progress

3. Perceived vs. True Nature

- Struggles can be chances to shape our character by teaching us valuable lessons.

2. The Wisdom ofStruggles

1. Self-Discovery

- Struggles reveal our inner strength, perseverance, and ability to overcome challenges
- They disclose more profound facts about our values, desires, and limitations

2. Clarity of Purpose:

- Challenges help

reassess priorities and align with our genuine purpose

- They reveal what truly matters, removing superficial concerns.

3. Empathy and Connection

- Struggles generate compassion, allowing us to understand others' sorrow and build closer relationships.

4. Struggles: Sources of Guidance Inner Strength:

.Difficult situations educate us to trust our intuition and problem-solving skills.

2. Redirection:

Obstacles may indicate a need to change direction, providing guidance towards a better path

- "What seems like a setback is often a setup for greater things

4. SpiritualAwakening

- Struggles promote spiritual introspection, leading to a stronger connection with the self and the divine.

5. Turning Struggles Into Strengths

1. Shift Your Perspective

- View challenges as learning opportunities rather than obstacles
- Question: What is this attempting to teach me?

6. Build Resilience

1 • Practice mindfulness, gratitude, and self-care to improve your ability to overcome adversity

2. Embrace Vulnerability

- Recognise and accept pain as part ofthe process, allowing healing and progress to proceed.

7. Seek Support:

- Seek advice and encouragement from reliable friends, mentors, or spiritual guides.

Many people find their soul purpose after overcoming adversity such as illness, financial difficulties, or loss.

As I indicated in the preceding chapters that I learnt a lot from animals along myjourney, I found my Animal totem Eagle, Dogs, Butterfly, and Cats out ofthese let's, take an example of, butterflies.

- A butterfly must battle to emerge from its cocoon, developing the strength required to fly.

It symbolises change and transformation. It represents transition, letting go ofthe past, and allowing time to heal. It teaches us to be patient.

8.. Applying Wisdom from Struggles in Life .

Share Your Lessons:

- Use your experiences to motivate and guide others going through similar situations.

2. Be Gratefulfor Growth:

- Examine how challenges have developed your character and broaden your perspective.

3. Integrate insights:

- Apply lessons learnt to future decisions for continual progress.

You are the cosmic awareness. We feel that everything must be accomplished from an external perspective; however, it is as simple as becoming aware of your entire existence. The more conscious you are of your mental, physical, spiritual, emotional, light, and shadow aspects, the more aligned you will be. We are electromagnetic beings who can withstand a certain amount of cosmic light indirect proportion to the frequency that we emit. In layman's terms, let your heart lead you down the right path, let your emotions rise, and discover wisdom within you that you never knew you possessed. And I feel that wisdom might be referred to as cosmic consciousness. Take note of the screen's white background as you read these words. On one level, you recognised it had been there the entire time. On another level, you didn't since your mind was preoccupied with the text. The same holds true for our link to cosmic consciousness. You're already linked. You just don't realise it because you spend all of your time focussing on the objects in consciousness, causing you to miss consciousness itself. When I say "objects in consciousness," I mean thoughts, emotions, people, objects, situations, and so on. Every one of those objects arises in awareness; this is how and where they are perceived. It's like watching a movie and being told to just focus on the screen, rather than the colors and shapes that show there. In a matter of seconds, you would be distracted by the graphics on the screen and lose track ofthe screen itself. We lose track of consciousness because our minds are constantly occupied by objects. But the link is there, even though there isn't a connection. It's who you are. The more you practice being aware of being aware, the more you begin to home in on your true self—cosmic consciousness.

1.*Applying the Cosmological Lesson to Everyday Life* :

1. .View personal struggles as part of a biggerjourney, just as individual stars contribute to the beauty ofthe cosmos.

2 .Embracing Change:

- Understand that change, even when difficult, is a natural and necessary force for growth.

3.*Living in Alignment*

- Be aware ofyour impact on others and the environment .4.Develop Awe and 4.*Gratitude:*

- Reflect on the universe's majesty to foster humility and astonishment.

I spend the majority of my time stargazing in order to feel the positivity of the universe while also reflecting on my role in the universe and its unlimited possibilities. After 20minutes ofthis activity, my energy level is restored.

3. Real-WorldApplications ofthe Cosmic Lesson

- In nature,

A forest regenerates after a wildfire, demonstrating renewal through devastation

- Quantum physics,

Confirms spiritual truths by revealing fundamental connection . • In Human Endeavors, Great leaders typically overcome difficulties and create transformative influence.

- *Belief in the* Unseen:

Similar to how gravity shapes the universe, unseen factors such as love and hope shape our lives.

My unseen experiences have been blissful. In the event of a failure situation, I am always hopeful that something goodwill replace the worst, and I receive an answer through mediums or signals that something good was hidden behind the bad, so now I have a habit of accepting the situation regardless ofwhether it is good or bad because I know I am doing the right thing with the right intention, and it is the universe's responsibility to take care ofthat, which it does. The cosmic lesson reminds us that the universe is more thanjust the backdrop to our life; it is a profound guide and source ofwisdom. Its cycles, connection, and balance are timeless truths that can foster personal growth and harmony. We gain clarity, purpose, and a stronger connection to our surroundings when we align with the cosmic principles of unity, transformation, and limitless possibility. The great expanse ofthe cosmos has a message: we are both insignificant and eternally significant, individual-sparks in an endless, interconnected flame.

The cosmic lesson is not only about the stars, but also about ourselves.

CHAPTER 11
GLOBAL AND PHILOSOPHICAL PERSPECTIVES

As mankind navigates an era of unparalleled global interconnectedness, the relationship between pragmatic and spirituality gains increased significance. Practicality promotes progress and problem solutions,whereas spirituality provides depth, meaning, and oneness.

Together,they can illuminate paths to world harmony and personal fulfillment.

This chapter examines global and philosophical viewpoints on the balance of practicality and spirituality, highlighting their roles in tackling humanity's difficulties and building a common vision for a peaceful future.

1. Spirituality and practicality in global contexts:

- Different civilizations around the world have their own ways of combining practical deeds and spiritual ideals.

- In India, *karma yoga* (selfless action) bridges spiritual devotion with practical service.

Ironically, they are not different. But the way we have been conditioned to conduct our lives, regardless ofwhich religion we follow, has led us to believe that you can only be spiritual or worldly and not both. But the truth is that both materialism and spiritualism may co-exist. It is possible to do both THIS and THAT. Being spiritually linked allows you to experience quantum leap progress in your worldly objectives since you now have GOD on your team to achieve what you believe is possible with your unique combination of born talents and acquired skills. Life has a design and laws that govern it. By adhering to these principles, we can excel in all aspects of our lives. You acquire more clarity in what you want to do once you are in a CALM and SILENT state ofyour MIND. Many thoughts converge to one thought and progressively There is no mental state that allows you to become AWARE of your BEING; instead, a voice within talks to you to show you the way and tell you what to do next; this is what Meditation is all about: connecting with your soul to help you fulfill your unique objectives and mission in the world.

Spirituality is not leaving the world and fleeing to the bush to seek SELF or GOD by avoiding your responsibilities/duties; ifyou do, you are an ESCAPIST rather than an SPIRITUALIST. Being in the world, being true to your individuality/spirituality, and attaining your worldly aspirations with a greater purpose in mind, as well as enjoying the pleasures and luxury of life, is truly spiritual and worldly. Allow this to coexist within you, and you'll understand how to balance it.

2. Globalisathon ofSpiritual Practices:

- Practices such as yoga, mindfulness, and meditation have spread globally. • These practices demonstrate the universal relevance of spiritual tools for dealing with personal and societal difficulties.

- Spiritual principles, such as compassion and interconnectedness, offer a shared language for fostering global unity amid cultural diversity.

- Spiritual values like compassion and connectivity provide a common vocabulary for promoting global harmony among cultural variety.

3.Science and spirituality are two sides ofthe same coin:

Modern science, including quantum physics and neuroscience, is increasingly aligned with spiritual conceptions of connectivity and consciousness . •

Philosophical considerations arise, including whether spirituality may accompany scientific study to address global issues

- Are they complimentary approaches of understanding reality?

2. Universal Ethics:

- Universal ethics are built on shared spiritual principles like truth, compassion, andjustice.

- Philosophers such as Immanuel Kant and spiritual leaders like the Dalai Lama emphasize the importance of balancing personal morality with global duty.

4. SocialJustice Movements:

Activism based on spiritual ideas aims to combat global inequalities by promoting values such as dignity, inclusivity, and collective wellbeing

- For example, Martin Luther King Jr.'s civil rights campaign was based on spiritual nonviolence and practical change techniques.

Bridging the Gap Between Practicality and Spirituality:

- Living as global citizens entails combining practical action and spiritual awareness to confront common concerns

- For example, participate in environmental activities while being grateful for nature's richness

- Spiritual qualities such as mindfulness, compassion, and simplicity can result intangible benefits such as less stress, improved relationships, and sustainable lives.

- Integrating spiritual principles into educational systems promotes holistic development, preparing students to manage difficult global situations with insight and creativity.

- Reflecting on the vastness ofthe cosmos inspires humility and unity, reminding us of our shared existence on a fragile planet.

- Just as the universe operates on the principles of balance and connectivity, humanity may achieve harmony by combining practical endeavours and spiritual insights.

OBSERVATION THROUGHOUTMYJOURNEY

The worldwide and philosophical viewpoints on practicality and spirituality reveal a significant truth: these two energies are not opposed, but rather complimentary. They work together to help us live more purposefully in an increasingly linked and complex environment. By embracing the lessons of many cultures, the wisdom ofgreat minds, and the expanse ofthe universe, we may bridge the gap between reason and faith, action and contemplation, material progress and spiritual fulfilment. The path to a balanced society begins with merging practicality and spirituality in our own lives, then spreads outward to alter the global community.

Practicality and spirituality are the two wings that allow humanity to soar toward a more peaceful and enlightened future.

CHAPTER 12
DIVINE MESSAGE: TO EVERYONE

Beloved souls,

You are more powerful than you know, more loved than you can fathom, and more linked to the infinite than words can convey. You are a one-of-a-kind representation ofthe divine, placed here on purpose rather than chance.

Within you is a sacred light that may illuminate not only yourjourney, but also the lives of people around you.

..You are Enough:

You were designed with purpose, and nothing about you is a mistake. Your abilities, as well as your problems, are all part of a larger plan to help you grow and realize your mission. Stop doubting your worth; you are perfect as you are.

..You are Connected:

You're never alone. Though the world appears to be fragmented, every soul, living entity, and the universe itself are inextricably linked. Every thought, word,and action creates ripples in the fabric of existence. Your love, generosity, and efforts, no matter how modest, generate ripples of positive change.

..*Love Is YourEssence:*

At your core, you are Love. When you feel lost or troubled, come back to this fact. Give love freely to yourself, others, and the planet. Love heals wounds, bridges divisions, and expresses the divine.

..Embrace Change

Life is constantly changing, much like the tides and seasons. Do not be afraid of change; it is the driving force behind your evolution. Even in times of uncertainty or pain, keep faith that all is going to plan. The difficulties you endure are lessons that will lead you to greater strength and wisdom.

THE END IS THE BEGINNING.

..*Be Present :*

The past is behind us, and the future awaits. The only reality is now. Every moment is a gift, an opportunity to appreciate beauty, be grateful, and make a difference. Live totally in the present moment—that is where the divine resides.The past is behind us, and the future awaits. The only reality is now. Every moment is a gift, an opportunity to appreciate beauty, be grateful, and make a difference. Live totally in the present moment—that is where the divine resides.

. ... You Have a Purpose:

Your existence is meaningful, and your unique gifts are required in the world. Whether your goal is to create, teach, nurture, or simply be, know that you are addingto the immense symphony of existence. Seek what makes your heart sing and then pursue it with courage and faith.

...Trust in the Better Plan :

There is a divine intelligence overseeing the universe and yourjourney

within it. Though you may not always understand why things happen, accept that everything is part of a larger plan for your personal development and the greater benefit.

...Serve and Shine:

You are here to serve, not in servitude, but as a brilliant person who spreads your light to others. Be generous with your generosity, tolerant with others' problems, and unwavering in your integrity. When you serve from the heart, you connect with the divine and accomplish your highest purpose.

... SeekBalance:

Strive to be in harmony with yourself, others, and the natural environment. Balance your mind, body, and soul; give and receive; work and relax. The divines flows most easily through a life lived in harmony.

...Remember YourDivinity:

You are more thanjust a body and mind; you are an everlasting soul, a spark from the infinite. Remember this reality when you're feeling doubtful or afraid. Meditate, pray, or simply breathe deeply to reconnect with the divine spirit that is constantly present inside you.

...watch your actions:

Action speaks more than words. Words and acts both have equal impact, but the action shows it. Be careful what you do and always choose what is right. Do not love with words or speech, but with acts and the truth.

.Stoodfor righteousness:

Live in a way that is right with God and follows my commands. It entails seeking holiness while avoiding sin in one's thoughts, words, and actions.

....Go Forward in Love and Light

Keep this message in your heart: You are here to grow, love, shine, and inspire. You are never isolated from the divine since it exists within you and all around you. Trust in yourself, yourjourney, and the limitless love that holds you.

You are supported by the entire cosmos. The divine believes in you. The world is waiting for your light.

With infinite love,

THE DIVINE PRESENCE

ACKNOWLEDGMENT

<u>Firstly</u> I'd like to thank God for providing me with the best parents and, of course, the best brother that any youngster could ever hope for.

<u>Secondly</u>, A big embrace to my grandparents, who always shower me with blessings from heaven and are always there to protect me, as well as my Nana and Naniji, who are still living and send me blessings from afar.

<u>Thirdly</u>, God chose my friend to help me overcome a difficulty while writing and selling my first book.

<u>Fourthly</u>,My mother helped me recognize that I am a wonderful writer and that I should write and share something uplifting.

<u>Fifthly</u>, My father, who is my role model, has always encouraged me to persevere in difficult situations and taught me to be honest, loyal, and devoted to everyone, including my work.

I am grateful to Author Inspiring Jatin, my mentor, who guided and pushed me to write my first book.

Finally, butjust as importantly, I want to thankyou for choosing this book and taking charge of your enlightened quest to bridge the gap between religion and reason. I'm confident that after reading this book, you'll begin to become more spiritual and logical and steer clear of any unpleasant obstacles in your path to enlightened living.

Remember to send me a note explaining how this book aided you and your loved ones during your trip. Kindly provide your Amazon reviews. Like you, a lot of others will be inspired to purchase this book and lead lives free from obstacles.

LOVEYOUALL....
PRAGATI BANGWAL
E-mail-authorpragatibangwal@gmail.com

www.ingramcontent.com/pod-product-compliance
Lightning Source LLC
LaVergne TN
LVHW061559070526
838199LV00077B/7104